Go-To Guides

A GIRL'S GUIDE to the

PERFECT SLEEPOVER

by Marne Ventura

CAPSTONE PRESS
a capstone imprint

Snap Books are published by Capstone Press,
1710 Roe Crest Drive, North Mankato, Minnesota 56003
www.mycapstone.com

Library of Congress Cataloging-in-Publication Data
Cataloging-in-Publication Data is available from the Library of Congress website.
ISBN: 978-1-5157-3663-9 (library binding)
ISBN: 978-1-5157-3668-4 (eBook PDF)
Summary: Crafts, games, and activities for sleepovers

33614080241309

Editorial Credits
Brenda Haugen and Abby Colich, editors; Juliette Peters, designer; Laura Manthe, production specialist; Morgan Walters, media researcher; Sarah Schuette, photo stylist; Sarah Schuette and Marcy Morin, project creators

Photo Credits
Capstone Studio: Karon Dubke, cover, 1, top left 4, 5, 7, 9, 11, 13, 15, 17, 19, 21, 23, 25, 27, 29, 31; Shutterstock: Africa Studio, 2, 3, bestv, (water bottle) 22, bigacis, 10, Darrin Henry, bottom right 4, Dionisvera, (black olives) 16, eurobanks, (travel kit) bottom28, Gumenyuk Dmitriy, (bubble) background 22, Jourdan Laik, (pens) 20, Madlen, (ball) background 20, Madredus, 1, Maren Winter, (vanilla bottle) 8, MaxShutter, (fabric) background 28, MG-PicturesProd, 14, nareerath, (saitn) background 6, 7, nchlsft, (tie die) background 26, Nomad_Soul, 12, Pamela D. Maxwell, (food coloring) 22, (muffin tin) 24, markers 26, Pefkos, (mint leaves) background 8, Pitpilai, background 30, 31, Ron Dale, (glitter) background 5, 32, Tom Wang, (tomato) background 16, Trinet Uzun, 18, ZanozaRu, (peppers) background 24

Printed in Canada.
010040S17

TABLE of CONTENTS

Get Ready for Fun!

A sleepover is a great reason to get together with friends. There are so many possibilities for things to do!

Do you like to dance? Teach your friends a new dance. *Is crafting a favorite hobby?* Plan a fun craft project to do. Hosting a sleepover is your opportunity to be creative! This book has tons of activities and projects to make your sleepover a fun time that your friends will remember.

Plan on a Good Time!

Planning your party is half the fun. Here's a list to help you get started.

- **Talk to your parents**, and decide on the number of guests to invite.
- **Pick a date that makes sense.** Be sure there's nothing big planned the next day.
- Will you **find what you need for games and decorations around the house** or will you have a budget to buy supplies for the party?
- **Send invitations** by mail or email, or deliver them by hand. Make sure your invitations include the date and time of the party, your address, and your phone number. Tell your guests if the party has a theme and if you would like them to bring anything. Give them a deadline to RSVP.

On the day of the party, have your decorations and food ready before your friends arrive. Welcome them at the door, and show them where they'll be sleeping. Make sure everyone is comfortable. Explain any rules your parents have given you. Then relax and have fun!

Sweet Dreams Photo Booth

Set the slumber party mood with this easy project. It does triple-duty as a party decoration, a fun activity, and a way to create a keepsake of your special night. It's easy to make, and you might even find the perfect supplies around your house.

You will need:

- navy blue sheet
- 6 thumbtacks
- scissors
- 1 sheet of white or colored card stock for each prop
- markers
- clear tape
- 10-inch (25.4-cm) bamboo skewers (1 for each prop)
- white glue
- glitter
- 24-inch (61-cm) length of ribbon for each prop
- camera or smart phone

Step 1

Hang the sheet from a wall so the bottom edge reaches the floor. Tack at even intervals across the top edge for your photo booth backdrop.

Step 2

Cut the cardstock in half to make 8.5-inch x 5.5-inch (21.6-cm x 14-cm) rectangles. Round off the corners with the scissors.

Keepsake Frames

Print your favorite pictures from the photo booth, and trim to 3-inch (7.6-cm) squares. Glue the pictures to the centers of 4.5-inch (11.4-cm) squares of cardboard. Glue a double row of craft sticks around the edges for a frame. Decorate with paint, markers, adhesive jewels, glitter, or stickers. Glue a ribbon to the top for hanging.

Step 3

Use the markers to write messages on the cards, such as "Sweet Dreams," "Slumber Land," "zzzzz," or "Good Night."

Step 4

On the backside of one cardstock prop, use clear tape to attach a bamboo skewer for a handle. Squirt a line of white glue around the edges and the top of the skewer where it touches the card. Add a second cardstock piece to make the backside of the prop.

Step 5

Squeeze a line of white glue around the edge of the cardstock prop. Sprinkle with glitter. Dry completely. Tie the ribbon in a bow around the handle, just under the card. To stop the bow from slipping, add a strip of clear tape on the backside.

Step 6

Have your friends (wearing pajamas, of course) hold a card and pose for a photograph in front of the backdrop. Take a group photo too!

TIP: If you'd like, hang a "Sweet Dreams" banner across the top of the backdrop, and stick silver stars to the sheet. Set a basket nearby filled with sleep masks, fuzzy slippers, pillows, and robes.

Delicious Lip Balm

Who doesn't need more lip balm? Gather around the kitchen table for this fun project. Guests can choose their favorite flavor and decorate the container lids with their own special touches.

You will need:

- jar of petroleum jelly;
  a 3.75-ounce (106-gram) jar makes 12
- small, screw-top containers
- craft sticks
- vanilla, mint, and lemon extract
- toothpicks
- white paper
- pencil
- scissors
- paper towels
- glue stick
- markers

Step 3
Place the container lid on a sheet of white paper, and trace around it. Cut out the circle just inside the trace marks.

Step 4
Wipe away any jelly from the outside of the container, and screw on the lid.

Step 5
Glue the paper circle on the lid, and decorate the lid with markers.

Step 1
Scoop the petroleum jelly into the screw-top container with a craft stick.

Step 2
Add a drop or two of extract. Mix well with a toothpick.

TIP: Find inexpensive screw-top containers at your local dollar store, discount store, or art supply store. Containers made of unbreakable materials, such as plastic or tin, are good choices.

Manicure Cookies

Here's a fun twist on a tried-and-true sleepover activity—a manicure you can eat! Start with ready-made cookie dough for ease and speed. Mix up frosting in your favorite colors while the cookies bake and cool. Paint your nails, pour some milk, and enjoy dessert.

You will need:
- baking sheet
- refrigerated sugar cookie dough
- cooking spray
- flour
- cutting board
- rolling pin
- butter knife
- spatula
- wire rack
- vanilla frosting
- several small dishes
- food coloring
- plastic knives, toothpicks, or craft sticks
- sprinkles and other edible decorations

Step 1
Preheat the oven and prepare the baking pan according to the cookie dough package instructions.

Step 2
On a floured cutting board, roll out the cookie dough.

Step 3
Ask an adult to help each guest take a turn tracing around a clean hand on the dough with a butter knife. Carefully move the cutout to the baking sheet, leaving 1 inch (2.5 cm) between cookies.

Step 4
Bake as directed on the package. When done, use a spatula to move the cookies to a wire rack. Cool completely.

Step 5
Divide the frosting into several small dishes. Add food coloring to each dish to make red, pink, or any other nail polish color you like.

Step 6
When the baked cookies are completely cool, use a knife, craft stick, or toothpick to give your hand a manicure. Don't forget a pretty ring on at least one finger!

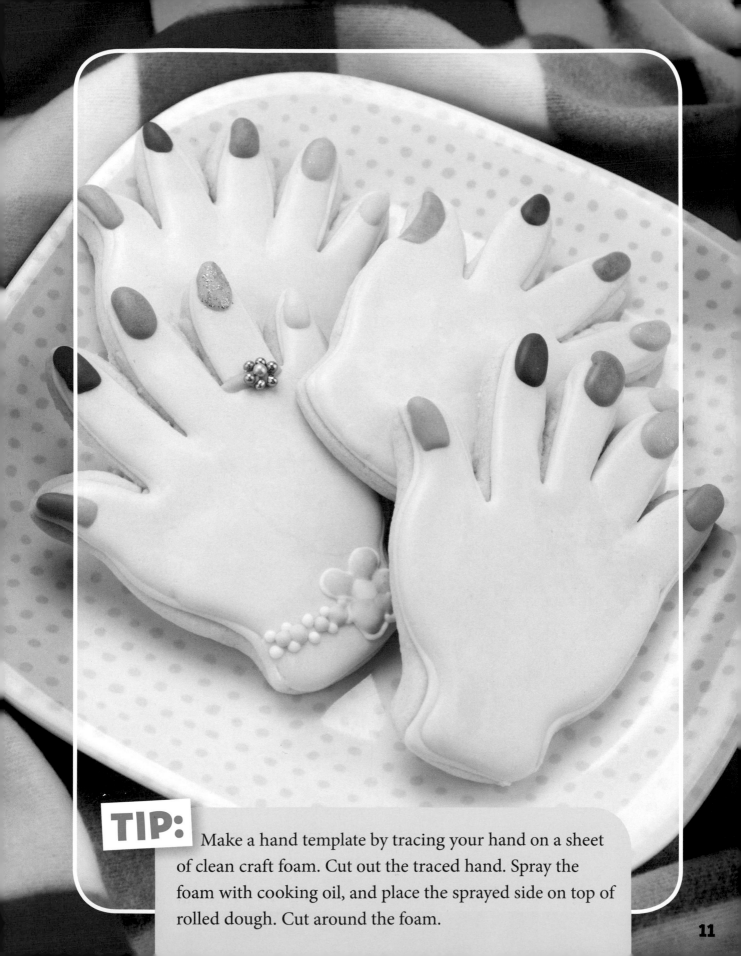

TIP: Make a hand template by tracing your hand on a sheet of clean craft foam. Cut out the traced hand. Spray the foam with cooking oil, and place the sprayed side on top of rolled dough. Cut around the foam.

Dream Catchers

Decorate your sleeping area with an American Indian folklore theme. This pretty wall hanging will add color and flair to your party. All you need are wire rings, a handful of yarn and string, plastic or wooden beads, and sturdy paper.

You will need:
- scraps of yarn or string in several colors
- 6-inch (15-cm) wire ring for each dream catcher
- scissors
- glue gun
- feathers
- plastic or wooden beads

Step 1

Tie one end of a length of yarn to the ring. Wrap the same yarn around the ring in three more places to form a star inside the circle. Cut the end.

Step 2

Add a dab of hot glue to hold the four corners of the square in place on the wire circle. Cool completely.

Step 3

Tie the end of a new length of yarn to the middle of one of the sides of the square. Repeat to form a second square inside the first. Repeat until the circle is filled.

What Is a Dream Catcher?

American Indians made dream catchers from natural materials such as twigs and feathers. They hung them over the cradles of babies to help them sleep peacefully. According to folklore, bad and good dreams float in the air at night. The web-like center of the dream catcher traps bad dreams. The hanging feathers send good dreams down to the sleeper.

Step 4

Sandwich the end of a length of yarn between two feathers, and glue in place. Tie to the lower edge of the ring.

Step 5

String beads and feathers onto lengths of yarn. Tie to the lower edge of the ring.

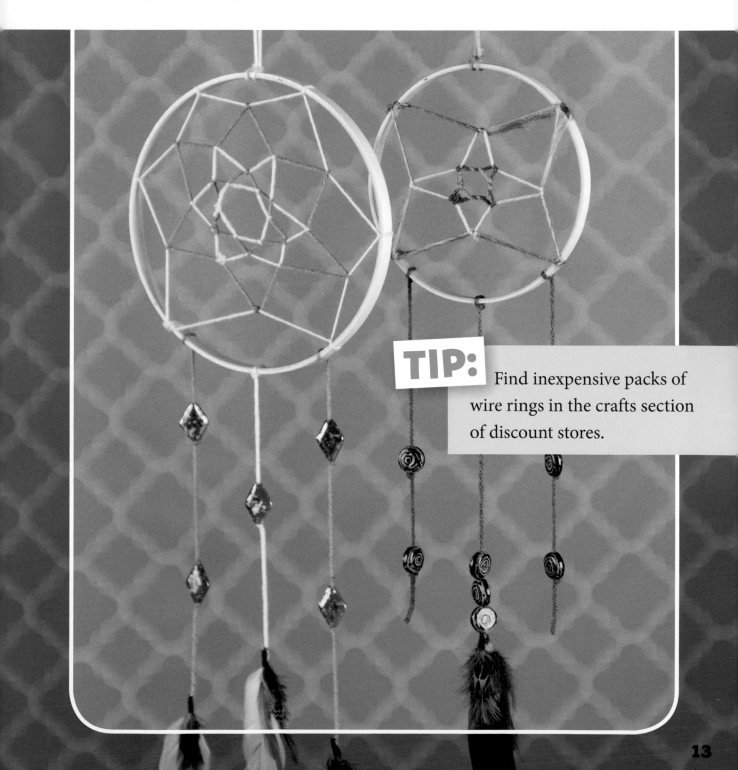

TIP: Find inexpensive packs of wire rings in the crafts section of discount stores.

Glow-in-the-Dark Lanterns

Plan to do this project right before you crawl into your sleeping bags. Clear jars with lids, glow sticks, and a bit of imagination are all you need to create a fun atmosphere after lights-out. These lanterns are quick and easy to make. They provide just enough light for munching popcorn while you watch your favorite movie.

You will need:
- clear pickle or jelly jars with screw-on lids
- hot, soapy water
- glow sticks
- paintbrush
- glue
- glitter

Step 1
Wash the jars in hot, soapy water to remove the labels. Rinse and dry.

Step 2
Paint the inside of the jars with glue. Pour in enough glitter to stick to the glue. Let dry completely.

Step 3
Bend the glow stick to activate the light.

Step 4
Place the glow stick so it fits into the jar. Screw on the lid.

Glow Stick Know-How

A glow stick has a glass tube inside of a plastic tube. When you bend or snap it, the glass tube breaks. This lets chemicals from the inner tube mix with chemicals in the outer tube. When the chemicals combine, they make light. Be careful not to cut or break open a glow stick. The chemicals inside can hurt your skin.

TIP: These lanterns make a great lamp if you take your sleepover outside. Try using plastic water bottles instead. They are just the right size and are not breakable.

Portrait Pizza

Everyone likes pizza. But what if one guest wants peppers and olives, and another wants pepperoni and onions? Let them add their own toppings, and everyone will be happy! Just for fun, make your individual pizzas look like faces.

You will need:
- baking sheet
- aluminum foil
- English muffins
- pizza sauce or tomato sauce
- shredded mozzarella cheese
- cutting board
- paring knife
- black olives
- bell peppers
- zucchini
- cherry tomatoes
- red onions
- carrots
- pepperoni
- parmesan cheese

Step 1
Preheat the oven to 375°F (190°C). Line the baking sheet with aluminum foil.

Step 2
Split the English muffins, and arrange them on the baking sheet.

Step 3
Spread some sauce on each muffin. Sprinkle with shredded mozzarella cheese.

Step 4
Cut the vegetables and pepperoni into shapes to make eyes, nose, mouth, and eyebrows. Use your imagination—the sillier the better!

Step 5
Sprinkle the toppings with grated parmesan cheese.

Step 6
Bake for about 10 minutes or until the cheese is brown and bubbly.

TIP: Instead of English muffins, try refrigerated biscuit dough. Flatten the dough with your fingers to make a 6-inch (15-cm) round crust. Add toppings, and bake at 400°F for 10 minutes.

17

Fancy Hair Holders

Next time you finish off a roll of giftwrap, save the cardboard tube. It's just right for making trendy ponytail holders with your friends. This project also uses recycled magazines and a technique called decoupage.

You will need:

- scissors
- cardboard giftwrap tube
- newspaper
- white glue
- water
- measuring cup
- plastic or paper cup
- paintbrush
- old magazines
- hole punch
- dowels (one for each hair holder)

Step 1

Cut the tube into 1-inch (2.5-cm) rounds. Cut a slit into each round.

Step 2

Cover your work surface with newspaper.

Step 3

Put ¼ cup (59 mL) of white glue and ¼ cup (59 mL) of water in the plastic or paper cup. Mix with the paintbrush.

Step 4

Cut out colorful pictures or patterns from old magazines or greeting cards.

Step 5

Cover the cardboard round with the glue mixture, and apply the cut-outs. Overlap the edges until the outside of the cardboard is covered. Paint a second coat of the glue and water mixture over the cut-outs. Let dry.

Step 6

If you'd like your hair holder to be shinier, add another coat of the glue and water mixture. Dry completely.

Step 7

To make your hair holder fit more tightly, punch holes in either side of it. Ask an adult to cut the dowel down to 3 inches (7.6 cm). Insert the dowel through the holes.

TIP: Scrapbooking rub-ons from the craft store would be cute on these! First cover the cardboard with white acrylic paint.

Ball of Questions

Sleepovers are a good time to learn more about your friends. This game gets the conversation going! Everyone gets a turn to talk and to listen. You think up the topics, so you can make them just right for your guests.

You will need:
- a large, inflatable beach ball
- a permanent marker

Step 1

Blow up the beach ball.

Step 2

Use the marker to cover the ball with questions. Here are some ideas:
- Cats or dogs?
- Favorite movie?
- Pizza or hotdogs?
- Favorite subject in school?
- Long hair or short hair?
- Favorite vacation spot?
- Dream job?

Step 3

Sit in a circle with your friends. Toss the ball to the person sitting across from you.

Step 4

The friend who catches the ball looks at the question closest to her right thumb. She has to answer that question.

Step 5

Players continue to toss the ball and answer the questions.

Step 6

Make sure everyone gets a turn. See the the conversation leads!

What is your favorite food?
Least favorite school subject?
What do you want to be?
What 3 words best describe you?
Cat or dog?
Inside movie or outside movie?
Favorite store?
Dream vacation?
Long hair or short hair?
What is your middle name?
Math or Science?
Pizza or hotdog?
What makes you smile?
Day or night?
Pet monkey or pet snake?
Winter or summer?
Favorite movie?
How tall do you think you will be?

Lava Lamps

Want a groovy sleepover? Make lava lamps! Recycle a clear bottle with a screw-on lid and a few other supplies from around the house. You and your friends can make one together for the party, or you can each make one to keep. Turn out the lights and enjoy the bubbles.

You will need:
- clear plastic bottle (any size) with a screw-on lid
- water
- vegetable oil
- food coloring
- effervescent tablet, broken into 4 pieces
- flashlight

Step 1
Wash the bottle in hot, soapy water to remove any labels. Rinse and dry the bottle.

Step 2
Fill the bottle one-fourth of the way full with water.

Step 3
Add enough oil so that the bottle is almost full.

Step 4
Let the water and oil separate. Add six drops of food coloring.

Step 5
Drop in one piece of the effervescent tablet in the bottle.

Step 6
For a more glowing effect, shine a flashlight through the bottle.

TIP: Make your lava lamps at a table covered with newspaper to catch any spills. Once your lamp is finished, screw the lid on tightly and wipe the outside clean before you move it. When your bubbles settle down, add another bit of effervescent tablet.

Fun Frittatas

You and your friends will be hungry for something delicious when you wake up in the morning. This easy frittata recipe lets everyone choose their own add-ins so they get just what they want. The savory egg muffins are fun to make together and taste great whether they're piping hot or room temperature. Add some fresh fruit and a slice of toast. This recipe makes enough for 12 people.

You will need:
- cooking spray
- muffin tin
- mushrooms
- green bell pepper
- zucchini
- 6 eggs
- ½ cup (118 mL) milk
- ¼ teaspoon (1.42 g) salt
- dash of pepper
- 1 cup (125 g) shredded cheese
- bacon bits

Step 1
Preheat the oven to 350°F (178°C). Spray the muffin tin.

Step 2
Dice the mushrooms, bell pepper, and zucchini into small pieces, and set aside.

Step 3
Mix the eggs, milk, salt, pepper, and cheese.

Step 4
Let each guest fill a muffin cup about one-third of the way full with her choice of fillings.

Step 5
Add the egg mixture so that the muffin cups are almost full.

Step 6
Bake for 20 to 25 minutes, or until the eggs are firm.

TIP: You can make these before the party if you'd like. Store them in the refrigerator and let your guests warm them in the microwave for 30 seconds to 1 minute when they wake up.

Flower Power Pillowcases

Tie-dye is cool, but this project is even more awesome! Skip the mess, and use colored permanent markers and rubbing alcohol to get the tie-dye effect. Ask your friends to bring a pillowcase to the party, or supply them yourself as a gift.

You will need:
- clean baking sheets
- 1 white, 100 percent cotton pillowcase for each guest
- colored permanent markers
- droppers
- rubbing alcohol
- clothes dryer
- iron
- ironing board

Step 1
Insert a baking sheet into the pillowcase. This will keep the colors from soaking through to the other side.

Step 2
Use markers to draw flowers on the front of the pillowcase. Remember that the ink is going to spread out when you add the alcohol. A simple pattern, such as a larger dot in the center with smaller dots around it, will bleed into a flower shape.

Step 3
Use the dropper to add rubbing alcohol to your marker designs. Go slowly, and stop when your ink has spread enough.

Step 4
Let your pillowcase dry completely. Then put it into the dryer for 15 minutes.

Step 5
Iron the pillowcase to set the colors.

Step 6
Your pillowcase is ready for sleeping! The colors are set, so it's okay to wash and dry.

TIP: A sheet of corrugated cardboard will work instead of a baking sheet. To help the pillowcase dry faster, add some paper towels under the top layer. This technique works on 100 percent cotton T-shirts too!

Sleepover Survival Kit

Wouldn't it be nice to have everything you need for a sleepover in one place? With this handy roll-up holder, your toothbrush and travel-size toiletries are ready to grab-and-go. This would be a fun project to make with your friends at a party. It would also be a nice gift to make ahead of time and give to your guests as a party favor.

You will need:

- 1 washcloth for each kit
- ruler
- sewing needle
- thread
- 2 feet (61 cm) of ribbon for each kit
- toothpaste, a toothbrush, hair holders, and travel-size toiletries for each kit

Step 1

Fold the washcloth so that one edge is about 2 inches (5 cm) below the other.

Step 2

Sew the two short outside folded edges together.

Step 3

Sew the fold at even intervals to make five pockets.

Step 4

Fold the ribbon in half, and sew the center of the ribbon to the center of one edge of the washcloth.

Step 5

Fill the pockets with toothpaste, a toothbrush, hair holders, and travel-size toiletries.

Step 6

Roll the washcloth up, and tie it closed with the ribbon.

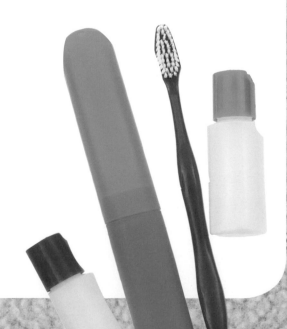

TIP: You can use a sewing machine instead of hand-sewing. Or you can use fabric glue to make the pockets, and skip the sewing altogether.

Pajama Bag

Do you have a favorite T-shirt that doesn't fit anymore? You don't have to say goodbye! Grab a pair of scissors, and make yourself a quick and easy sleepover tote. It's just the right size for your pajamas and toothbrush.

You will need:

- scissors
- T-shirt (any size will work, but the bigger the T-shirt, the bigger the bag)
- ruler
- recycled cardboard
- pen or pencil
- round plate or lid
- permanent fabric marker
- felt
- fabric glue

Step 1

Cut the hem off of the bottom of the T-shirt.

Step 2

Cut a 5- x 0.75-inch (12.7- x 2-cm) cardboard pattern. Use the pattern to mark lines along the bottom of the T-shirt. Make sure the front and back of the T-shirt are lined up. Cut through both layers to make fringe.

Step 3

Cut a U shape through the front and back of the neck: First, place a plate or lid at the base of the neck hole. The bottom of the plate should be even with the base of the armholes on the sides. Trace around the bottom half of the plate. Use a ruler to draw a straight line from the sides of the plate to the shoulder of the shirt on each side. Cut through both the front and back of the shirt on the lines.

Step 4

Cut the armhole sides in a deeper curve to match the curve of the neck.

Step 5

Start at one side. Tie the front fringe to the back fringe in a knot. Continue across the bottom until all the front fringes are tied to the back fringes.

Step 6

Insert a piece of cardboard between the front and back so the ink won't go through. Write "SLEEPOVER" on the front with fabric marker. You also can use fabric markers to create fun designs on your bag, such as hearts or other shapes. Or you could cut star and moon shapes out of felt and use fabric glue to add them to your bag. Use your imagination to make your bag unique.

TIP: Pick a T-shirt with a team logo or pretty print, and skip the permanent fabric marker and felt.

Read More

Bolte, Mari. *Unique Accessories You Can Make and Share.* Sleepover Girls Crafts. North Mankato, Minn.: Capstone, 2016.

Jones, Jen. *Planning Perfect Parties: The Girls' Guide to Fun, Fresh, Unforgettable Events.* North Mankato, Minn.: Capstone Press, 2014.

Turnbull, Stephanie. *Fun with Friends: Style Secrets for Girls.* Girl Talk. Mankato, Minn.: Smart Apple Media, 2014.

Watson, Stephanie. *Plan a Sleepover Party.* Party Time! Minneapolis: Lerner Publications Company, 2015.

Internet Sites

FactHound offers a safe, fun way to find Internet sites related to this book. All of the sites on FactHound have been researched by our staff.

Here's all you do:

Visit *www.facthound.com*

Type in this code: 9781515736639

Check out projects, games and lots more at
www.capstonekids.com